Ink & Insight

Adhiti Mukund

BookLeaf Publishing

India | USA | UK

Presentation by *BookLeaf Publishing*

Web: www.bookleafpub.com

E-mail: info@bookleafpub.com

ISBN:9789360949600

First edition 2024

To One Direction,

*For the melodies that filled our hearts and the
lyrics that became our anthems...*

ACKNOWLEDGEMENT

I am deeply grateful to everyone who has contributed to the creation of this book.

First and foremost, I want to express my heartfelt appreciation to my family and friends for their support and encouragement throughout this journey. Your love has been my anchor, and I am thankful for your belief in me.

A special thank you to all my teachers, whose wisdom and guidance have been invaluable. Your insights have helped shape this collection in ways I could never have imagined.

I am also indebted to the countless writers, poets, and artists whose work has inspired me over the years. Your creativity has fueled my own, and I am grateful for the beauty you bring into the world.

PREFACE

Welcome to INK AND INSIGHT! Before you dive in, I want to share a bit about what inspired these words.

Poetry has always been my sanctuary—a place where I can express the feelings and thoughts that swirl within me. Each poem in this book is a piece of my heart, a glimpse into my inner world.

These verses were born from moments of joy, sorrow, love, and contemplation. They were crafted with care, each word chosen to evoke emotion and spark imagination.

As you read through these pages, I invite you to join me on a journey of discovery. May these poems speak to you in their own unique way, offering solace, inspiration, and perhaps a bit of magic.

Thank you for embarking on this poetic adventure with me.

Warm regards,
Adhiti Mukund

Moonlit Path

Silver beams upon the ground,
Lighting up the path I've found.
In the quiet of the night, I roam,
Finding solace, far from home.

Drifting down from the wintry sky,
Each snowflake unique, none defy.
Blanketing the earth in pure white,
Nature's art, a wondrous sight.

Colors blend, in the evening sky,
A masterpiece before the night.
Slowly fading, as darkness falls,
Beauty in endings, nature \calls

Diamonds scattered across the black,
Guiding lost souls, leading them back.
In the vast expanse, dreams take flight,
Underneath the starlit night.

Overgrown with weeds and moss,
A path once taken, now at loss.
Memories fade, footsteps erased,
Yet in the heart, its echo embraced.

Shadows

Shadows chase her
Her beauty unhazed
Does dark retract
When she lets the sun beam her rays?

Or does she follow
Behind trees, clouds and lamps
Hiding in the hollow
Waiting for the day

The day the sun rewinds
The moment she goes no further
When she smiles at the darkness
And no longer tries to disperse her

Skipping stones

Skipping stones on water's grace,
Ripples fade without a trace.
Each pebble tells a story bold,
Of dreams lost and stories untold.
Across the stream, the pebbles glide,
Secrets buried in the tide.
Each skip a journey, far and wide,
In the water's flow, we confide.
Yet in the stillness, echoes ring,
Ripples fade, but memories cling.
Each pebble, a chapter, a tale to tell,
In the stream of life, we dwell.
So cast your pebble, let it fly,
In the stream of life, let it lie.
For in its journey, truth you'll find,
In the ripples left behind.

Art of letting go

Like autumn leaves, falling to the ground,
Sometimes we must let go, to be found.
Shedding layers of the past, to make room for
the new,
Embracing change, in all that we pursue.
It's not easy to release what we hold dear,
But in letting go, we conquer fear.
For in the emptiness, lies boundless space,
For new beginnings, to find their place.
So let go of what no longer serves your soul,
And trust in the journey, to make you whole.
For in the art of letting go, we find release,
And in release, we find peace.

Wilted roses

Petals fall like tears in rain,
Beauty fades, yet love remains.
Wilted roses, still hold grace,
Memories linger in their embrace.
In the garden, roses weep,
Wilted petals, secrets keep.
Each bloom a story, buried deep,
In the petals, dreams may sleep.
So cherish every rose that blooms,
Hold it close, in its perfume.
For in its beauty, find your light,
Wilted roses, still shine bright.
And when the petals start to fall,
Wilted roses, hear their call.
For in their fading, love does grow,
Wilted roses, forever show.

Nature calls

The sun is bright
Rain always light
Birds flying around, and nothing is too loud
The cloud kingdoms stand so high
Majestic and enticing
Like those birds, I wish I could fly
For this dull life is tiring
Take me away, I say,
up there is where I belong!
My arms I flail but to no avail
I shall look all day long.
The sun being bright fills my heart with delight
Time has slowed down
My soul no longer frowns

Lost swan

The moon shines brightly
In the night sky as always
But tonight, sadness fills the air,
For the swan, once graceful, isn't there.

Wall to wall

Wall to wall,
the concrete climbed.
Highs and lows
that which flows
bricked to my mind.

Birds, Breeze, Beautiful things

Birds, Breeze, Beautiful Things:
A bright sunflower up above
A chemistry of cells flickering in between
Cursed with prohibited love
A butterfly with a sacred past
And a moth with the presence of hope
A connection that was meant to last
With anxiety that could cope
But all this was just a fantasy
While the beautiful night starts to cry
The light starts going down the drain
The soothing voice begins to lie
And time slowly starts filling with pain
While sleep is just death being shy
Misery will overtake love

Love is easy to say goodbye
Until a butterfly comes by again

A journey through words

Words upon a page grasped close in my hand
A gateway to another realm, a journey
unintentional
I avoid myself in the tale's embrace.
As reality fades, leaving no trace.

Characters and plots come alive.
With each turn of the page, I'm hypnotized.
On a planet of illusion, of love, and of pain
I find myself dreaming of a book's landscape.

The pages whisper mysteries untold.
As my anxious eyes continue to behold
I'm taken to a world so new.
Somewhere, far from the ordinary race

With each word, my imagination runs free.
Creating a world just for me

I feel like a trailblazer on a never-ending
crusade.
With every chapter, I get more and more
captivated.

The smell of the pages, the melody of the spine
The touch of the words makes it all feel divine.
I'm lost within the book; my spirit does sing.
Forgetting my worries and overlooking the
entirety

In this book, I find my solace.
As I delve deeper, my mind takes a pause.
It's an interim escape from the anarchy outside.
A refuge of peacefulness, where I can hide

The feeling of getting lost in a book
Is there something I can never disregard?
Inside those pages, there's a realm to explore.
And I'll keep getting lost forevermore.

If I could fly

If I could fly
I could reach mountaintops
I would soar high into the heavens
Past the clouds
Past the sky as it forms a gradient to black
Past the stars
I would soar to the heavens
But why stop there?
If I could fly
I would rise to the heavens
But I would return
From high above
Because home
Is where we can truly feel love

Golden

The sun rays glistened,
Golden,
The world heard and listened
To the chirping.
With cold wind blowing,
The air's still crisp;
And you caught a glimpse.
As the planet of love smiles
To you who cries.

Blue sky reverie

and all day,

I dance upon this world,

I swirl in a daunting delight,

and I listen, I listen

to the wind compose a most beautiful poem,

I feel a thousand words upon this aching skin

under the arch of a blue, blue sky

as it sags, as it breaths,

and I dance,

I dance with my fingers and my soul,

I dance in this beautiful skin

and I feel myself as a poem

under the arch of a blue, blue sky

do I feel the poem of a God?

and all day long, I lift to the sky,

plaster my hands upon its ancient skin,

and I listen, I listen,

to the sky as it whispers a lost lullaby,

I tilt upon my toes,

lean my ear in,

and I hear the lumbering procession of a most
beautiful universe pass by,

so I dance, I dance and I dance

and I intricate a most articulate orchestra with
this body,

with this world,

and in an instance,

I feel the song of a universe bloom in this body

Crimson Twilight

As the sun sets
And as flowers bloom
As the winds blow
Set a time for doom
Things may be bright
Yet again who knows
The brightest angels
Have bitter flaws
As fire spreads
And as volcanoes erupt
As the ravens scream
This love may not corrupt
Not a single wicked scheme
Has ever been seen
In the hearts of most wicked
Love has been

The moon

He shines, luminating the gloomy sky
Cold, stern, huge he stands there hovering over
mankind
His soft glow ignites a fire inside of me
Keeping me warm whether i wanted to be
The loneliness that once was there
Disappears when i admirably stare
Into his beautiful beam
As if its all just a dream
But coldness quivers my heart
When he suddenly departs
Behind the gloomy clouds
Out of my bounds
Oh how does a single moon
Bring one so much fortune?

A promise

I saw you,
Saw you in the night sky
Shining with the tiny stars
You stood up there
Shining and shining
With the light of a thousand stars
The night sky reminds me of something
And brings a sourness in my heart
Oh! There's something I wanted to say
But I'm just too afraid
Too afraid it'll make you sad
So I'll not say it
Not say it now
But I'll tell you, someday or the other
That's for sure
That's a promise between you and me
For promises are never to be broken
Just wait till that day comes

And I shall tell you
Because that's a promise
A promise I made to you

Silence of the night

The lights hum and the wind whispers
But it's so unbelievably quiet.
No noise no sound no movement no...
No Nothing.
The clock waves in silence, barely ticking
Half the speed, calm, gentle clicking.
This goes on for hours, or many a few seconds.

Rain gently pumels the ground creating a thin
layer of hope.
Quiet.
Peacefully, the wind seems to hammer at the
houses.
The light seams to hide behind the branches
But its quiet.
No planes, no machines no talking, no...
Absolutely nothing.

Empty?
Perhaps, with the day so busy, the morning so
bright
The night is now lonesome, no proof of
anything.
Quiet.
I really feel it.
Dainty taps of the leaves on the window panes,
distant voices in sleepy houses.
But still.
It's so, so quiet.

Dark and light

In olden times, where shadows hide their might,
Among the battle between dark and light,
A silent war goes on, unseen by day,
Where honor fights the sly in its way.
With quiet plans, the tale doth show its might,
In simple words, fate takes flight.

What will go with it?

What will it go with
And what remains here,
Say you,
Came I here with nothing
Shall I go with nothing,
Isn't it?

Triumph against turmoil

Where thunder meets the ground,
A brave heart wanders through the haze,
Through tests and shadows,
he finds his light,
With trusted friends, he takes the flight,
a journey where courage prevailed.
where stars aligned,
A hero emerges
one of a kind.

Tale of 5 men

here is a tale of 5 men
one of them drifted
leaving hearts wounded
some heal
some never stay the same
the next one built a new town
paving path
to a new home
third's a charm
he managed to grow
and turn the growing pain into flowers
the other one picked a different road
and killed his old self
to become a butterfly
and the last one's on his way

slowing the ride down
becoming a man of his own
while staying in his roots